RETRIEVAL PRACTICE: RESOURCE GUIDE

Ideas & activities for the classroom

KATE JONES

JOHN CATT
FROM HODDER EDUCATION

Every effort has been made to trace all copyright holders, but if any have been inadvertently overlooked, the Publishers will be pleased to make the necessary arrangements at the first opportunity.

Although every effort has been made to ensure that website addresses are correct at time of going to press, Hodder Education cannot be held responsible for the content of any website mentioned in this book. It is sometimes possible to find a relocated web page by typing in the address of the home page for a website in the URL window of your browser.

Hachette UK's policy is to use papers that are natural, renewable and recyclable products and made from wood grown in well-managed forests and other controlled sources. The logging and manufacturing processes are expected to conform to the environmental regulations of the country of origin.

Orders: please contact Hachette UK Distribution, Hely Hutchinson Centre, Milton Road, Didcot, Oxfordshire, OX11 7HH. Telephone: +44 (0)1235 827827. Email education@hachette.co.uk. Lines are open from 9 a.m. to 5 p.m., Monday to Friday.

ISBN: 9781913622541

© Kate Jones 2021

First published in 2021 by
John Catt from Hodder Education,
An Hachette UK Company
15 Riduna Park, Station Road,
Melton, Woodbridge IP12 1QT
Telephone: +44 (0)1394 389850
www.johncatt.com

A catalogue record for this title is available from the British Library

'Before you start something new, review the old.'
Paul A. Kirschner

CONTENTS

INTRODUCTION

I have written a lot about retrieval practice in recent years. Undeniably, it is a topic that interests me a lot. There are two reasons why I continue to be so passionate about retrieval practice: evidence and experience. Firstly, the research surrounding retrieval practice is positively overwhelming. It dates back over a hundred years and research continues to be carried out in classrooms and laboratories around the world. I aim to be an evidence-informed teacher and leader, accepting research cannot give us all the answers but it is also far too important to ignore. Secondly, my own classroom experiences have shown me the positive benefits and impact that regular retrieval practice can have on both the student and the teacher. I have seen increased confidence with my students as well as feeling more confident in myself as a teacher too. I have observed a clear improvement in terms of outcomes and results. I am convinced this strategy has a place in the classroom and it is not just me that thinks so, there continues to be widespread interest and enthusiasm around retrieval practice.

In my previous books, I have explored and discussed academic research as well as conducted interviews with leading academics in this field however, this book is quite different. It focuses simply on providing the classroom teacher with practical retrieval practice resources, ideas and tools that they can try, adapt and use in their lessons. There is a visual example of each resource as well as a brief explanation as to how it can be used in the classroom alongside some of my top tips. There are ideas in this book from my previous books too as I am aware not all readers will have read my other books. I am also aware there will be familiar readers too so I have ensured there are plenty of new ideas that can be introduced into classroom practice.

Due to the outbreak of coronavirus and its disruption with school closures and lessons becoming virtual, I have also included a range of free quizzing tools that can be used for online retrieval practice. Retrieval practice should take place every lesson, whether that is in the physical or virtual classroom. Thank you to all the teachers that have allowed their retrieval practice ideas to be included in this workbook. I hope you find this book helpful and useful. If you have any feedback or questions you can contact me on social media or via my website lovetoteach87.com.

CHAPTER 1:
RETRIEVAL PRACTICE TASKS IN THE CLASSROOM

Like many other teachers, I regularly start my lessons with a retrieval practice task. It has become an established routine in my classroom which has contributed to it being accepted and even expected by my students, adding to the low stakes element of retrieval practice. Whilst I do advocate starting every lesson, or most lessons, with retrieval practice I also want to stress that retrieval practice shouldn't be limited to the start of a lesson. I haven't encountered any academic research that states retrieval practice should be used at a specific point. It really can be used at any point in a lesson.

We need to strike the balance between allowing enough time for retrieval practice with meaningful feedback and reflection but also not let retrieval practice tasks hijack our lessons when we have new content to deliver. Fortunately, retrieval practice is very flexible and all of the tasks in this chapter can be adapted for different classrooms. When I found I was rushing feedback because too much time had been spent on a task, I decided to reduce the amount of questions. Regular review and reflection are key here.

My teaching mantra consists of taking an approach to planning and delivering classroom tasks that are low effort, high impact. The low effort refers to tasks that don't require hours of cutting, sticking and laminating and can support teacher workload so that time and effort can be invested elsewhere, whether that be developing subject knowledge or having a better balance in our lives. The high impact refers to student learning and this part is essential. I am an advocate for promoting a love of learning but I know previously my students have completed tasks that, on reflection, I would describe as engaging but empty – they didn't have the desired impact on learning I intended. Tasks can be enjoyable and engaging but they *must* be effective when it comes to long-term learning. When you are implementing these ideas in your classroom keep in mind 'low effort' and 'high impact'.

BIG QUESTIONS

Big question: What were the aims of the 'Big Three' with the Treaty of Versailles?	Big question: What were the military terms of the Treaty of Versailles?
Big question: What were the economic terms of the Treaty of Versailles?	Big question: What were the effects of the Treaty of Versailles on Germany?

How it works: If you use 'big questions' or key/enquiry questions as part of your learning intentions shared at the start of a lesson then a useful idea is to revisit these later with a retrieval task. Learning intentions should be long term, after all it is only when time has passed that we can check if information has been learned and can be recalled from long-term memory. This can be in a grid or table format or simply just revisit one previous 'big question' and find out what students can or cannot remember.

Top tips: Aim to focus and include 'big questions' that link in with the new material being introduced and taught in the lesson. Take the example above of the big questions referring to the Treaty of Versailles. The lesson it could be used in might include a big question about Hitler's rise to power as, ultimately, the Treaty of Versailles contributed to that.

COPS AND ROBBERS

Your own knowledge and recall...	Information you have 'stolen' from your peers...

How it works: The 'Cops' column is for students to write as much as they can from memory about a specific topic or previously covered material in a set amount of time – similar to a brain dump (see page 57). Once the students have had about four to five minutes to write as much as they can from memory they then have to complete the 'Robbers' section. This is where everyone in the class needs to get out of their seats and read their peers work, swapping and sharing their ideas and content.

Top tips: If you are using this activity with younger students you can add columns with subheadings to provide more structure and guidance in terms of what information students should be recalling. This is shown in the example on the following page and is credited to Emily Folorunsho for adapting the original Cops and Robbers activity.

Factor	Your own knowledge and recall...	Information you have 'stolen' from your peers...
Victorian London		
Working conditions		
Living conditions		
Jack the Ripper		
Other key facts...		

EXPAND AND ELABORATE

Expand and elaborate	
Henry VIII had six wives	
Henry VIII broke from Rome	
Henry VIII dissolved the monasteries	

How it works: The teacher provides a series of facts or statements linked to previous content taught. The students then have to expand on that statement using their own knowledge from memory. The statement acts as a prompt, but the students are encouraged to elaborate and include as much detail as they can. This activity has the potential to be adapted to use with quotations (explaining the meaning or context of the quote) and key dates (asking students to explain what happened in that year) or with key individuals and so on.

Top tips:

- It can be a good idea to select examples to read aloud or perhaps show an example of a statement and the accompanying retrieval statement to model to students what is expected of them in terms of literacy, detail and explanation.

- This can be used in MFL to develop and combine writing skills and retrieval practice.

- The number of statements provided depends on how much time you want to allocate on this. At the start of a lesson, I find three or four statements that work well, allowing time for discussion, sharing and reflection. If I want students to go beyond a sentence and write sentences or a paragraph then I will reduce the number of statements to one or two.

FINISH THE ANSWER...

Question: Explain two effects of the Montgomery Bus Boycott on the Civil Rights Movement in the USA.

One effect of the Montgomery Bus Boycott on the Civil Rights Movement in the USA was that it led to the eventual desegregation of buses. This was achieved because...

Another effect of the boycott was that it led to further peaceful protests across America such as...

How it works: Students are given a sentence starter (or more than one) and then they must complete the rest of the answer. They don't need to copy out the original sentence as this can take up precious lesson time and is essentially a scaffold that will eventually be removed. The idea is that it acts as a prompt for them to recall, add and elaborate. This can be used with younger students as it provides support but it can also be used with older students with examination style questions.

Top tips: It's a good idea for students to swap and share their responses because, although they all had the same starting points, their answers can be very different. This is also helpful because they may see or hear information in their peers' responses that they didn't include in their response. This can easily be adapted by adding or removing support too.

INDIVIDUAL SPOTLIGHT

INDIVIDUAL SPOTLIGHT – MARTIN LUTHER KING

How would you describe this person?
Legendary, confident, leader, brave, non-violent, inspiring, intelligent

What is this individual best known for?
"I have a dream" speech

What other people are connected to this person?
Rosa Parks, NAACP, JFK, Coretta Scott, Lyndon B. Johnson

What other key facts can you recall about this individual?
MLK was religious, well educated and a great public speaker.

Create a question where the key individual is the answer.
Who led the Montgomery Bus Boycott?

SELF ASSESS YOUR UNDERSTANDING OF THIS PERSON IN RELATION TO OUR TOPIC: GOT IT! ALMOST! NOT YET!

How it works: This recall activity focuses on individuals, including monarchs, characters or people of significance in your subject. The activity can be easily adapted for each subject, focusing on the key aspects students need to be able to retrieve. You can include an image as a cue too. Often students can recall trivia facts or responses that lack depth, such as 'Henry VIII was fat'. This encourages more specific and focused retrieval.

Top tips: This task can be adapted to recall information about a range of individuals such as characters from the same text. An extension task could be to ask students to explain any links and connections between the individuals.

LABEL IT

How it works: This naturally works better in some subjects than others. If students need to be able to identify and recognise key features of a diagram then it is useful to provide the diagram without any labels. In a history lesson, I could give my students an image of a WW1 trench and they would label the key features. This has potential in geography, maths, science and many practical subjects too.

Top tips: You can add further prompts and support by adding the first letter of the label, so for a trench duckboard I may include the letter D. To make this more challenging the arrows can be removed so students must find for themselves what needs labelling. You could also ask students to explain the key features while they are labelling.

LIST IT

Ysgol (School)	Bwyd (Foods)	Hobiau (Hobbies)
• Hanes	• Afal	• Rygbi
• Mathemateg	• Siocled	• Pel droed
• Saesneg	• Te	• Rhedeg
• Cymraeg	• Coffi	• Nofio
• Gwyddoniaeth	• Bara	• Dawnsio
• Athro	• Cawl	
• Gwaith dosbarth	• Moron	
• Llyfrau	• Bisgedi	
• Wisg ysgol	• Crempog	
• Amser cinio	• Sglodion	
• Addysg Grefyddol	• FFa pob	
• Miwsig	• Hufen ia	
• Celf	• Pys	
• Technoleg	• Reis	

How it works: This is great across a range of subjects. This resource example is from a Welsh language lesson where a student has had to recall lists of school subjects, foods and hobbies. This is an opportunity to interleave topics. The 'list it' approach isn't restricted to vocabulary as key terms, dates, events, characters, themes and quotes can also be listed.

Top tips: Encourage students to swap with each other and share their lists, adding anything they have collected from their peers in a different coloured pen. For higher-order thinking, this task can be linked to elaboration or making connections with the factors in the list.

MINI WHITEBOARDS

How it works: We know how mini whiteboards (MWBs) are used in the classroom but they aren't always used as effectively as they could be. MWBs are great for asking questions in class and ensuring everyone is involved in the retrieval process. Questions asked could be multiple-choice questions or questions which require brief answers, such as key dates and key individuals or characters. Students can also illustrate their answers too.

Top tips: Do not ask questions that require extended answers as it will be incredibly difficult or impossible for the teacher to scan a class and read each answer. Keep it minimal – that is why multiple-choice or keyword answers are ideal. The teacher can then provide immediate feedback and further discussion.

MISCONCEPTIONS RETRIEVAL
by Rachel Ball

Misconception	Correct or better answer? Try and use explicit evidence where you can.
In Medieval England, public health everywhere was very poor.	
The development of anaesthetics such as chloroform was immediately useful in improving medicine.	
Rich people and royalty experienced better medical treatment than the poor during the Renaissance.	
Governments during the 1800s were not concerned about public health in towns and cities.	

How it works: The teacher will write a collection of misconceptions, these can be general misconceptions based on previous classroom experiences or from classwork. The misconceptions will often be points that students can find confusing, get wrong or aren't necessarily true. The students have to then rewrite, correct or improve the original statement.

Top tips: Rachel has said: 'This is a great thought process to go through as a teacher, particularly after an assessment or the reading of books before whole-class feedback. This got my students thinking and provoked a really good discussion.'

PICTURE PROMPT

Explain in your own words, from memory, how each icon is linked to what we have studied about Henry VIII:

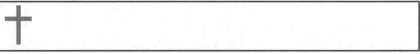

How it works: This is another very simple activity that works well with younger students as they require more support and guidance with recall. Each icon/image will be a prompt and cue for the students to write or type what they can from memory. Instead of simply asking 'What can you recall about Henry VIII?', this task supports students to be more specific with their recall. I have found that the quality of student answers improved significantly through the use of prompts as support.

Top tips: Use the website nounproject.com for icons to include, they have over three millions icons that are ideal for this task, but make sure it is clear what the icon represents as this can cause further confusion. In terms of photos, you can use pixabay.com to download copyright free, high-quality images at no cost but again ensure they are relevant.

RETRIEVAL BASKETS
by Patrice Bain

How it works: This task does not require baskets, that is simply what the author and teacher Patrice Bain uses. The idea is that in a lesson the teacher and/or students will write down questions based on the content of that lesson. The questions are then added to the basket (which can easily be substituted by an envelope or tray) and this can be added to each lesson. The questions won't be answered in that lesson, instead wait for some time to pass then revisit the questions in the basket. The teacher can ask the questions via a strategy such as cold calling – a Doug Lemov 'no hands up' technique where the teacher will call on any student in the class to answer – or questions can be given to students to answer independently.

Top tips: It is not easy for students to write questions that have a desirable level of challenge therefore it is always useful to model examples of retrieval questions when asking students to create their own.

RETRIEVAL GRIDS

Rank the following in order of importance with reasoning for *Othello*: passion, malice, vulnerability.	Give two examples of *Othello* critical analysis or of *Othello* intertextuality.	How is artifice and reality depicted in *Othello*? Support with evidence.	Rank the following in order of importance with reasoning for *Streetcar*: passion, malice, vulnerability.	Which theme is the poker game in *Streetcar* most significant for: power, time or sensuality?
Give specific examples of Greek mythology utilised in every text studied this year.	Explore Stella's position in the play with supporting quotes.	How significant is light and darkness in *A Streetcar Named Desire*?	State the importance of the title *History* and link to another poem.	How are men other than Iago and Othello presented in the play? Why?
How is Emilia presented throughout the play? How important is her role in the drama?	How are secrets presented in *A Streetcar Named Desire*? Support your answer with evidence.	State two 'Poems of the Decade' that would reinforce themes of modernity.	Define 'kitchen sink drama' with an example from *A Streetcar Named Desire*.	Give one contemporary intertextual quote to demonstrate views on Othello's race.
Explore the characterisation of Blanche in *A Streetcar Named Desire*.	Do any poems deal with a sense of 'rebirth'? If so, which? Ensure you have quotations.	'Iago is the central character of *Othello* above the eponymous hero', explore your perspective.	Name three poems where youth is an important theme and justify with quotations.	Which poems would most strongly tie to the themes of brutality? Give supporting evidence.

■ 1 point - Last lesson ■ 2 points - Last week ■ 3 points - 2 weeks ago ■ 4 points - 3 weeks ago

Credit to Jancke Schwartz (@awakenenglish) for the English literature retrieval grid

How it works: This is a self-explanatory resource. Retrieval grids are one of my most popular and versatile resources. This is because it can be easily adapted across all subjects and key stages. This activity promotes spaced retrieval practice and can be used for interleaving topics too. To make this task truly no stakes you can remove the points, even with points it can be low stakes as students should focus on their scores and their personal bests rather than competing with others. You could also replace the questions with headings or prompts.

Top tips: If you wish to use this at the start of a lesson then simply ask four questions that cover the last lesson, last week, two weeks ago and further back. This enables the class to write more in-depth answers while allowing time for meaningful feedback and reflection.

RETRIEVAL PLACEMAT

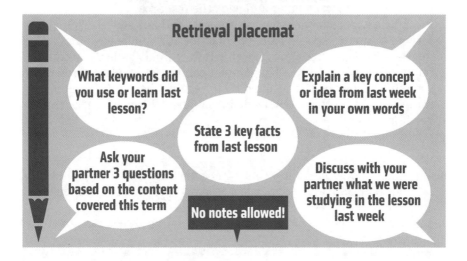

How it works: The aim of the retrieval practice placemat is to promote verbal discussions amongst peers about previously covered content and, of course, retrieve that information from memory by doing so. As the questions are generic this removes subject-specific cues and prompts to make it more effortful and challenging. The generic questions can be used across a range of subjects and with different classes.

Top tips: Laminating the placemats will ensure they last longer in your classroom or alternatively as a paperless option you could simply project the placemat onto the board as a slide for students to read and discuss. Personally, I have found this to be a more convenient option as I am not always based in the same classroom.

RETRIEVAL PYRAMID

4 points

Explain how *Blood Brothers* illustrates the issue of social class.

3 points

Explain how superstition and fate are key themes in the play.

How do Mrs Johnstone and Mrs Lyons know each other?

2 points

Who wrote *Blood Brothers*?

What does it mean that Mrs Johnstone lives on the never never?

Which character said 'Now y'know the devil's got your number'?

1 points

What are the names of the Johnstone twins?

In which city is *Blood Brothers* set?

Which character guides the audience through the story?

How do Mrs Johnstone and Mrs Lyons know each other?

How it works: The key difference between the pyramid and the grid is that instead of the retrieval questions varying in terms of when content was taught, the questions vary in terms of their difficulty. At the bottom are easier questions, which all of the class should be able to confidently answer as a way to provide retrieval success and boost their confidence. Higher up the pyramid, the questions will become more challenging. Unlike previous differentiation tasks, this idea allows everyone in the class to be challenged and have the opportunity to be stretched.

Top tips: The pyramid can be used as a way to scaffold questions, starting with basic factual recall and building up to more complex, higher-order thinking questions. Again, points can be removed to be truly no stakes. This could be adapted with more or fewer questions, depending on how much time you wanted to dedicate in a lesson to this task.

RETRIEVAL REGISTER

How it works: Taking the register is a great opportunity for students to complete a settler or 'do now' style activity. It can also be an opportunity to involve everyone in the class in a retrieval task. Instead of the teacher asking a question for each student, the teacher will ask the class to tell them a key piece of information about a specific topic. When a student's name is called they must state their fact. The teacher may even want a student to elaborate on an answer or point. Students cannot repeat something that has already been said.

Top tips: Don't always start the register at the same point as the first person will always have it easy based on their position within the register. Start from the top, another time start from the bottom or even part way through a register. It can be helpful to tell the class you will be doing this next lesson and tell them the topic in advance. If they are concerned about trying to recall information on the spot in front of their peers this gives them the time to prepare and be ready with a range of key facts. This can be done both in the physical or virtual classroom.

RETRIEVAL RELAY RACE

Retrieval relay race!

Instructions: In the first box **write as much as you can remember** about our topic. In the second box, one of your peers must write what they can recall about our topic **but they cannot repeat any of the information from your first box!** The third box needs to be completed by someone else but again this must include new information and the same again for the final box.

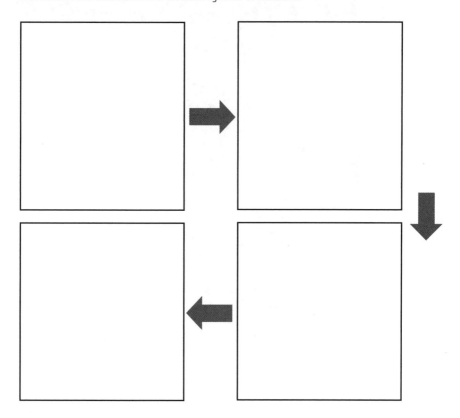

How it works: This task is designed to promote retrieval but also stretch and challenge students to remember as much information as they can, as well as collaborating with others. Students will complete the first box on their sheet – the first leg of the relay – with the information they can recall. Then their peers complete the other three boxes, continually adding more information each time, with no repetition of content allowed so that the retrieval relay becomes more challenging with each box.

Top tips: This activity can take time as students will need to read each box before they retrieve information to ensure they don't repeat any points. This activity can be adapted digitally using collaborative online tools such as Google Docs.

RETRIEVAL ROCKETS
By Emma Turner

How it works: This is a retrieval strategy for the early years foundation stage and primary classes. There is a rocket with a specific number of stages to launch. Let us take five stages for an example. For the rocket to take off, students need to recall five key facts. This can be adapted from facts to words or any content relevant to the subject/topic. As Emma describes it in her lessons with students – remembering rockets!

Top tips: This activity can be carried out individually or members of the class can work together, for example in a group of five each person must recall one key fact each and they combine them for the rocket launch. Teachers can use a rocket prop or a digital version! It's great fun.

RETRIEVAL TENNIS

How it works: Do not panic – no tennis balls or racquets are needed! This is a verbal retrieval task completed in pairs. The idea is that there's a chosen topic and the pairs take it in turns to recall facts/information that is relevant to that topic. They cannot repeat themselves or say something that their partner has already said. They then go back and forth, recalling information. Scores can be kept but it should be low stakes. No stakes can be even better where the students aren't in competition but instead are trying to keep the retrieval volley going for as long as they can together.

Top tips: The topic can remain the same but keep in mind that it will eventually become more challenging as students will need to recall more information. Challenge is good but an alternative would be to alternate the topic. This can be done in class, break out rooms or using the chat functions.

WALKABOUT BINGO

Q. What is a person called when accused of committing heresy? A: Heretic Name: Abby	Q. Describe the crime of treason. A: Plotting against monarchy Name: Katie	Q. Name an item that was smuggled in the 17th and 18th century? A: Brandy, Silk Name: Sophie
Q. Give a cause of crime. A: Poverty Name: Beth	Q. State one reason highway robbery increased. A: Cheap guns Name: Owen	Q. State one reason highway robbery declined. A: Banks Name: David
Q. Who was the fictitious leader of the Luddites? A: Ned Ludd Name: John	Q. What did the Luddites damage? A: Textile machinery Name: Charlotte	Q. What was the name of the riot that happened in South Wales and saw men dressed as women? A: Rebecca Riots Name: Megan
Q. Describe living conditions in the 18th and 19th century. A: Awful Name: Robert	Q. Name a crime associated with technology. A: Hacking Name: Courtney	Q. Give an example of terrorism. A: 9/11 Name: Chloe
Q. Name a crime associated with motoring. A: Speeding Name: Miss K Jones	Q. Give a cause of crime from both the Tudor period and 20th century. A: Poverty Name: Graham	Q. How has technology helped prevent or solve crime? A: DNA Name: Adam

How it works: This task encourages students to talk to one another, going beyond the typical think, pair and share as they have to engage with different members of the class. It is very simple to create and also very adaptable. Students can only ask their peers one question each, they record their answer and name and then move on. The first person to have all answers filled in shouts bingo!

Top tips: This activity is one of my favourite classroom tasks. I love listening to students asking each other questions. To adapt simply amend how many questions are included on the sheet.

CHAPTER 2:
RETRIEVAL PRACTICE TASKS TO SUPPORT LITERACY

I spent the first six years of my teaching career at Elfed High School, Buckley in North Wales. I adore this school and feel very grateful for the opportunities and how much I learned whilst there. Literacy was a whole school priority at Elfed, as it should be. It was also made very clear that developing literacy skills was not the sole responsibility of the English department but instead all teachers – regardless of subject or key stage – had a duty to support students with their literacy, again as it should be. In my first book *Love To Teach*, there were two chapters I dedicated to literacy. I continue to learn a lot from others – such as author Alex Quigley – about how we can close the reading, vocabulary and writing gaps both inside and outside of the classroom.

Retrieval practice plays an essential role when developing students literacy skills. A lot of the retrieval tasks in this book provide opportunities for reading and writing. I have focused more on using retrieval practice to support vocabulary with subject-specific terminology, although this focus can, once again, be adapted to different subjects and key stages. I take real joy in listening to students recall information and use key terminology in the correct context and confidently, which retrieval practice helps students to do. I also enjoy reading students written responses where, again, they have used sophisticated subject terminology when recalling information from long-term memory. Regular retrieval practice linked to vocabulary can also support and improve spellings too.

A-Z OF KEYWORDS

A _____

B _____

C _____

D _____

E _____

F _____

G _____

H _____

I _____

J _____

K _____

L _____

M _____

N _____

O _____

P _____

Q _____

R _____

S _____

T _____

U _____

V _____

W _____

X _____

Y _____

Z _____

How it works: Although already a classic classroom resource, I wanted to include this because it works well as a retrieval activity and focuses on key terminology, as do many of the resources in this book. This can be used with students of all ages as my GCSE classes will often include terms such as *Reichstag, Diktat, Fuhrer*, etc. I don't let students do this in pairs, they do this on their own but I will use class discussion to ask students what terms they included after and students can add words to their list if they did not include them originally.

Top tips: I often wait to do this with my classes until the end of a topic as they will have a wider range of subject-specific vocabulary. Again, this can also be a good opportunity to model pronunciation and check spellings.

GO FOR GOLD

Write an overview of what you have learned so far. Aim to include the following keywords in your answer...

Bronze: Abdication | Revolution | Mutiny

Silver: Autocracy | Industrialisation | Armistice

Gold: Weimar Republic | Democracy | Constitution

How it works: This is another activity that encourages students to recall information and include subject-specific vocabulary in their answers. This is cued recall as the words provide a prompt and guidance as to what students should include in their responses. It's easily adaptable for different topics, subjects and ages.

Top tips: Ensure all the terms in the 'bronze' section are accessible for all. This will provide support, retrieval success and a boost of confidence for all learners. Aim to include very specific and more challenging terms for 'silver' and 'gold'. More or fewer words can be added, depending on how long you wish to spend on the task or how long the answers are expected to be, from a sentence to a paragraph or essay.

KEYWORD GRIDS

MANIFESTO	CAMPAIGN	ELECTION
DEMOCRACY	VOTE	CANDIDATE
PARLIAMENT	CONSTITUENCY	REFERENDUM

How it works: There are many ways to use this grid. You could ask students to define each word, explain how the keywords link, or even write an answer with the aim to include all of the following terms – either a sentence for each keyword or a paragraph including as many as possible. You could also use the method of asking what is the question if the keyword is the answer?

Top tips: This can also be a great opportunity to develop literacy skills. The teacher can model pronunciation of keywords. This can also support spellings too.

KEYWORD SPOTLIGHT

In your own words write a definition:

Democracy: A system with a government chosen by the people for the people fairly.

Use the term correctly in a sentence:

Countries that have a democracy include Britain, USA and Australia.

Create a question where the keyword is the answer.

What is the system where a government is chosen by the people?

Keyword: Democracy

What other words are connected to the keyword?

Election, equality, politics, democrat, political parties, government

Draw a or find a picture to illustrate this keyword:

SELF ASSESS YOUR UNDERSTANDING OF THIS KEYWORD: GOT IT! ALMOST! NOT YET!

How it works: This is another activity that can either be used for consolidation or retrieval depending on what stage of the teaching and learning process is taking place, also if there is support provided or not. The spotlight is on a subject-specific keyword and all the tasks on the sheet relate to that term. This can promote discussion in class with students sharing their definitions, examples, questions and other relevant keywords.

Top tips: If students can confidently complete all of the tasks then, generally, they self assess their understanding/recall as 'got it' or 'good' but some students still self assess 'almost' which is useful for the teacher.

ROLL AND RETRIEVE

	1	2	3	4	5	6
6	2 x 4	48 ÷ 4	12 ÷ 4	8 x 4	8 ÷ ? =2	36 ÷ 4
5	36 = ? x 4	3 x 4	Write out your 4x tables	What is 1/4 of 24?	6 x 4	3/4 of 16?
4	3/4 of 32?	28 ÷ 4	11 x 4	8 ÷ 4	28 grapes 4 children. How many grapes each?	4 ÷ 1
3		4 x ? =	32 children in a class are split into groups of 4. How many groups?	4 x 4	What is 1/4 of 12?	10 x 4
2			24 ÷ 4	44 ÷ 4	16 ÷ 4	40 ÷ 4
1			12 x 4	Apples cost 4p each. How much would 9 cost?	7 x 4	Can you find one quarter of 100?

How it works: This 6x6 grid is an idea originally credited to Steve Bowkett and I first discovered this activity in Andy Griffith and Mark Burns's popular book *Outstanding Teaching: Engaging Learners*. I have adapted this idea in many ways, including involving retrieval practice. A class set of dice are required to use the grids. In pairs or small groups, students roll a set of dice once, as they will need a number to use both vertically and horizontally. They then answer the question in that specific box, hence roll and retrieve!

Top tips: This can be a time-consuming activity as each of the 36 boxes require a question. A good idea is to find examples other teachers have already made or share and collaborate with others. Investing in soft roll dice is another handy tip for the classroom too.

THINKING AND LINKING GRIDS

	1	2	3	4	5	6
1	Scrooge	Light	Tiny Tim	Marley's chains	Memory	Forgiveness
2	Family	The Ghost of Christmas Yet to Come	Scrooge as a school boy	Martha Cratchit	Fan	Peter Cratchit
3	Gratitude	Christmas	Reform	Poverty	Cold	The Ghost of Christmas Past
4	Marley's ghost	The charity collectors	Bob Cratchit	Ignorance and Want	Mrs Cratchit	Generosity
5	Hope	The Ghost of Christmas Present	Compassion	The workhouse	Redemption	Fezziwig
6	Repentance	Isolation	Belle	Responsibility	Fred	Guilt

Links made

Box 1	Box 2	Link between the two

How it works: Students work in pairs, roll the dice and if the first set of numbers are 3 and 4 the students will explain how poverty links to the text. Students roll again and then have to try to link the first factor – in this case, poverty – with the second factor that is selected randomly again by the dice. The example on the previous page was created by Stuart Pryke (@SPryke2).

Top tips: Encourage students to share their connections with other members of the class. There are naturally some very obvious links but students have surprised me with carefully crafted connections they have made.

VOCABULARY CHASE

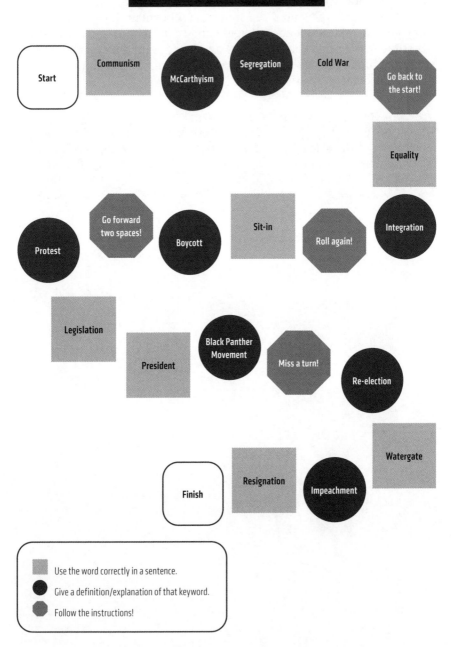

Start

Communism

McCarthyism

Segregation

Cold War

Go back to the start!

Equality

Go forward two spaces!

Protest

Boycott

Sit-in

Roll again!

Integration

Legislation

President

Black Panther Movement

Miss a turn!

Re-election

Watergate

Finish

Resignation

Impeachment

Use the word correctly in a sentence.

Give a definition/explanation of that keyword.

Follow the instructions!

How it works: This is an enjoyable and straightforward game where, again, the focus is on subject-specific keywords. Dice and counters are required to play vocabulary chase. Students roll the dice and based on the number, move their counter to that box. Each box has a keyword inside. The boxes are coloured coded with the instructions as follows:

Yellow = Use the word correctly in a sentence.

Red = Give a definition/explanation of that keyword.

Blue = Follow the instructions.

Top tips: This task can be used during the middle of the topic/course to check for understanding and as part of consolidation or once some time has passed and without any support for retrieval practice to occur.

VOCABULARY GRID

Roll a pair of dice and come up with keywords connected to our topic beginning with...

	1	2	3	4	5	6
6	A	J	I	D	F	B
5	H	K	B	W	R	I
4	Y	J	O	F	S	U
3	L	C	A	M	T	N
2	G	O	V	P	C	D
1	R	Z	S	E	S	T

How it works: This is another 6x6 grid but I like how this does not need to be adapted and can be used with all classes. Again, students complete this in pairs, they can either write down their keywords or say them verbally to their partner (there are benefits to both). I have used this with Year 7 classes where 'V' is Viking and Year 12 where 'V 'is 'Vagrancy'.

Top tips: As with most of the resources in this book you can download my template, see the QR code at the back of this book.

CHAPTER 3:
RETRIEVAL PRACTICE
WITH TECHNOLOGY

Any teacher who taught in the 2020/21 academic year will have likely taught lessons virtually. This proved a unique learning experience for everyone in the school community from teachers and school leaders to students and their families. Whilst I am sure you will agree with me that teaching in the online classroom is not as enjoyable as in person, in a classroom or a school building, there are lots of benefits to using technology for teaching and learning. When it comes to using technology for retrieval practice, teachers are spoilt for choice! There are a huge range of online and quizzing tools available which vary in terms of cost and quality. I have three golden rules I follow when using technology in the classroom and if I share a website or online tool with colleagues I check it passes my three rule test. The three rules are:

Low stakes – retrieval practice is a low stakes strategy for improving learning, not an assessment strategy. There are many great online tools that can be used for formal testing and assessment but I would encourage teachers to keep those tools separate from the day-to-day lessons and quizzes. There's plenty of choice so you can decide – either on your own, as a department or even at a whole school level – which tools work well for assessment and which should be kept for regular low stakes retrieval practice.

Workload friendly – this is one of the many benefits of technology that teachers need to take advantage of. Many of the quizzing websites I recommend and discuss in this chapter have various tools that can support teacher workload through pre-made quizzes or adapting existing questions so we don't have to design retrieval tasks from scratch. However, even if you wanted to design from scratch, you can save questions you have created to use again at a later date, supporting workload in the long term. Most online quizzing tools will provide instant feedback through results and scores to the students and teachers. This is super helpful and will save valuable time. We don't need to scrutinise the data of every retrieval practice quiz but we have that information at hand which can be insightful for future planning.

User friendly – for me this is the most important factor. I need to fully understand how a quizzing tool or website works so I can set the task for class, provide instructions, ensure I check they have completed it and view their results. Students also need to be able to use the website with ease so they can focus on the recall. If a website or tool is complex and difficult to navigate then it could be problematic in the classroom. We can avoid that scenario and stick to online retrieval practice tools that are user friendly – simple but effective.

All of the websites and tools in this chapter pass my test in terms of low stakes, workload friendly and user friendly. I am not an ambassador for any company or website. I only promote and share websites that I have used in my classroom or that other teachers have shared with me based on their positive experiences. No doubt, more online quizzing tools and websites will be created but again refer back to my three rules and ensure that question design is given careful consideration and regular review and reflection.

CAROUSEL LEARNING

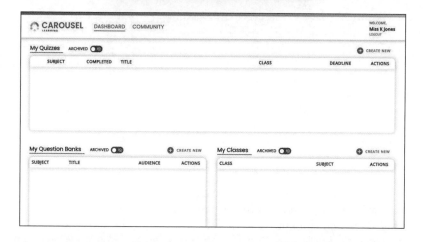

How it works: This online quizzing tool is based on the popular Retrieval Roulette, originally designed by teacher and leader Adam Boxer. You upload your retrieval questions on previously taught material. This online site uses sophisticated spaced repetition algorithms to select questions that will be asked over a period of time. It can also auto-mark questions too, saving time for the busy teacher. Visit carousel-learning.com to give it a go.

Top tips: Check out the existing question banks that teachers have uploaded and shared freely for others to use. This is great for collaboration but also great for easing teacher workload too!

GOOGLE FORMS

How it works: Google Forms are very versatile as a range of questions can be asked, including multiple-choice, short answer, paragraphs and the option to include a linear scale. There are templates available and quizzes can be copied and shared with other classes and colleagues, as well as setting deadlines too. Images and more can also be added too.

Top tips: This advice applies to any online quizzing tool but, at my school, we use Google Forms for formal assessments and online end of year exams. Therefore, our students associate Google Forms with being high stakes. If you do use a specific platform for high stakes assessment then use alternatives for the low stakes quizzing.

GOOGLE JAMBOARD

Countries were jealous of Britain because of their empire and navy. This caused a lot of tension!

There were two major alliances, meaning countries in the alliances would support the others if war broke out and that's exactly what happened. War broke out and the alliances dragged lots of countries into it.

The death of Franz Ferdinand caused even more problems between countries where tensions already existed, such as Austro-Hungary and Serbia.

Militarism involved countries competing to have the biggest and best army – how do you prove your army is the best? Go to war and win!

Nationalism is when you think your country is better than others and sometimes people were prepared to fight or die to prove this like Gavrilo Princip.

Kaiser Wilhelm was very jealous of England, he wanted to prove himself and show Germany was great.

The main causes of WW1 were militarism, alliances, imperialism, nationalism and the assassination.

The death of Franz Ferdinand angered Austro-Hungary a lot. This has been described as the spark that caused WW1.

There were some countries that had a lot of rivalry and tension such as the UK and Germany but other countries that supported each other in alliances such as the Triple Alliance and Triple Entente.

Germany and France were rivals, Germany and Britain were rivals but Britain and France were allies on the same side.

How it works: Google Jamboard is a digital canvas, like an online interactive whiteboard that is easy to use and is great for remote learning. Students can work and collaborate on the Jamboard. Up to 50 people can do so at once. Go to jamboard.google.com to give it a go.

Top tips: If you want to learn more about how to use Google Jamboard or any of the digital quizzing tools I have recommended, there are helpful short YouTube tutorials that can be viewed. Most are self-explanatory but it can help to watch a demonstration of how to use these tools before doing so.

KAHOOT

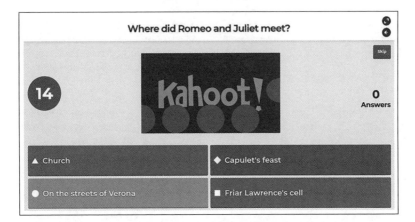

How it works: This was the first online quizzing tool I used in the classroom and, since then, it has become incredibly well known and popular in schools around the world. What's great is that Kahoot also continues to update its features for the classroom. As with most online tools, you can view other teacher's question banks. Previously, Kahoot only allowed teachers to use others quizzes, which I found problematic, but now it is easy to select and use single questions when searching through quizzes on your chosen topic.

Top tips: As with most online quizzing tools, I find the basic free package to work well. There are often options to upgrade with various prices. Slides can be imported from presentations as well as the option to include images that can be slowly shown with the image reveal feature. Visit kahoot.com to give it a look.

MENTIMETER

How it works: This quizzing tool is truly no stakes as students are not required to input their name. This might be frustrating for the teacher, as we are unable to see which responses match the students but it is useful for a snapshot overview of the class. Questions can include free recall or multiple-choice and there a range of features such as including relevant images as prompts. Go to mentimeter. com to set up your free teacher account and it is very easy to get started!

Top tips: Explore the WordCloud options. You can pose a question where students can only respond using single words. Mentimeter will then combine all of the responses into a class WordCloud.

MICROSOFT FORMS

Social Studies

UAE Quiz

...

1. Which of the following is the capital of the United Arab Emirates?

○ Dubai

○ Abu Dhabi

○ Muscat

○ I don't know yet

Submit

How it works: Naturally, schools that are using Google Classroom are using Google Forms too and those who prefer Microsoft Teams and functions are using this platform. The options include multiple-choice, short answer, ranking and long answers. As with Google Forms, questions can be selected so that they are required meaning students cannot skip the question. If questions are not required the students have the option not to respond.

Top tips: There is the option to include a rating which can be useful for students to self assess their level of confidence. Forms can be shared with colleagues. Responses can be viewed, deleted, printed or exported to Excel.

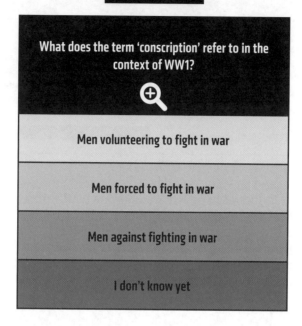

How it works: Through Quizizz, you can create your own quizzes from scratch or you can search the Quizizz library and use quizzes or questions made by other teachers. This is a low stakes, workload-friendly, user-friendly and fun online quizzing tool. You can include multiple-choice questions, free recall, create flashcards, add audio, images and much more to personalise your quizzes. It will provide you and your students with instant results. Simply sign up at quizizz.com and set up a teacher account.

Top tips: Quizizz can be personalised in lots of ways so it is worth exploring what this free site can offer. You can edit or remove question timers, keep or remove leaderboards and comical memes can be shown to students once they have answered a question – you can even upload your own memes too! It can be used in class or set as homework.

QUIZLET

Government	political institution that has the power to enforce rules and impose order and stability on a society. (It has the power to enact laws, execute justice, and enforce public policy).
	Click again to see the term ⬆

How it works: Quizlet has been around for a while and continues to be popular with teachers and students alike. It includes a range of useful features such as key term lists as flashcards, mini-tests, battles, matching exercises and the Quizlet live function. Quizlet promotes a lot of variety in terms of the task and question design. Visit quizlet.com to discover more.

Top tips: Quizlet also contains a wide range of pre-existing quizzes and flashcards that students can use. Quizlet ticks every box in terms of being workload and user friendly, as well as proving an enjoyable low stakes quizzing tool.

CHAPTER 4:
RETRIEVAL PRACTICE REVISION TASKS

I have to start this chapter by stressing that although retrieval practice is a superb revision strategy, it shouldn't *only* be used as preparation for examinations. It is a superb teaching and learning strategy. It can and should be used all year round, across all subjects and with learners of all ages. In addition to my head of department role, I teach GCSE and A Level and I'm a Key Stage 4 form tutor so I have supported students with exam revision from an academic and pastoral perspective – both being incredibly important. This is where pastoral and academic leaders can really work together as research has shown that regular retrieval practice can lead to an increase in confidence and decrease in student anxiety.

The work of Professor John Dunlosky and his colleagues has become relatively well known in education. Dunlosky *et al*[1] reviewed the efficacy of ten different learning strategies including those popular with students such as highlighting and re-reading. Dunlosky stated that, 'We rated two strategies – practice testing and distributed practice – as the most effective of those we reviewed because they can help students regardless of age, they can enhance learning and comprehension of a large range of materials, and, most important, they can boost student achievement.'[2]

Dunlosky is referring to retrieval practice with practice testing and distributed practice refers to what is more commonly known as spaced practice where study is spaced out over a period of time instead of massed practice – more commonly known as cramming before an exam! Spaced retrieval practice is highly effective so we need to ensure our students are doing this both inside and outside of the classroom. In order for students to embrace these strategies they need to fully

---

1. Dunlosky, J., Rawson, K. A., Marsh, E. J., Mitchell, N. J. and Willingham, D. T. (2013) 'Improving Students' Learning With Effective Learning Techniques: Promising Directions From Cognitive and Educational Psychology', *Psychological Science in the Public Interest* 14 (1) pp. 4-58.
2. Dunlosky, J. (2013) 'Study Strategies to Boost Learning', *American Educator.* Retrieved from: www.bit.ly/31jRkdM

understand the many benefits and also have a range of strategies and techniques that they can use independently. It is also important that parents and families are aware of the many benefits and the positive impact of effective strategies in comparison to those deemed to be less effective, such as highlighting and re-reading. These techniques often provide learners with a false and misleading sense of confidence and familiarity with content.

BRAIN DUMP

How it works: *'Write down everything you can remember about…'* It really is that simple. This is the ultimate low effort, high impact classroom activity! This task requires minimal planning from the teacher, apart from thinking carefully about what you are asking students to retrieve. This does require a lot of effort from the student as there is no support. This is free recall. More effortful can be more effective! This can be done with pen and paper or digitally on a document.

Top tips: Remember you can ask students to brain dump verbally to a partner instead of writing everything they can recall about a topic. The partner can then add further points or do a verbal brain dump for another topic.

FILL IN THE GAPS

Civil rights timeline: fill in the blanks, some key dates have been provided to help you.

1955		1963 "I have a dream..." speech delivered by MLK	1965	1968 Martin Luther King assassinated

How it works: I was never a fan of this classic classroom activity originally, the main reason being that I remember doing it in school and always found it too easy. It is a task that can be completed very quickly with minimal effort but with a desirable level of difficulty, which can be a useful retrieval activity. The example provided is a timeline with significant missing key events and dates that students will need to add. This isn't as easy as just guessing what word needs to be added. Fill in the blanks with sentences can still be challenging, especially when the blanks are specific key terms that students need to recall. This can also be useful for quotations. I have included two dates but left one box empty, this is challenging but also because there is more than one event, students could potentially add to that timeline.

Top tips: Don't make this too easy – if anything, focus on the challenge! There is already a lot of support and information provided so we need to make it challenging, to make students think and ultimately recall information from their long-term memory.

FLASHCARDS

How it works: Flashcards have been used for years but, as with most things in education, they can be used effectively or poorly. Students should not copy out notes onto flashcards. I have seen many students transfer information from the textbook to flashcards. They often look very impressive but they simply lead to re-reading rather than retrieval practice. We must explain and model to students how flashcards can be used effectively with questions and answers for retrieval practice.

Top tips: Flashcards don't need to be flashy! An effective flashcard should contain a desirably difficult question on one side and the answer on the other side. Tell your students to follow these simple steps: retrieve, reflect, reshuffle and repeat. There are lots of great online tools for flashcards including Quizlet and Anki.

FOLDING FRENZY
(by Simon Beale)

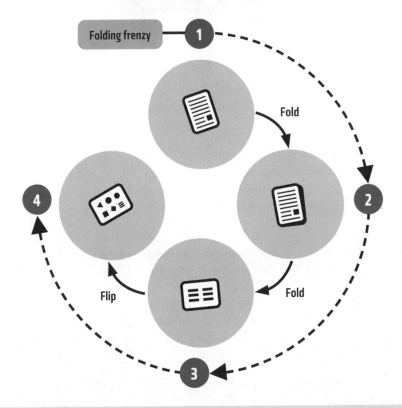

How it works: A folding frenzy is a multi-layered revision technique that uses a range of strategies in one package to rigorously encode and synthesise knowledge for better retrieval during exams.

1. Notes

Students write a page of notes on a piece of blank paper on a specifically chosen topic. Focusing on:

1. Key vocabulary
2. Summarising content
3. Using symbols

2. Graphic organiser

Students then create a graphic organiser representing the core terminology of the notes.

3. Flashcard

Students write down five or six keywords that summarise the topic.

4. Symbols

Students use the symbols from their original notes.

Top tips:

Students regulate their knowledge and understanding based on retrieval strength. They can then be kept in 'stacks'.

1. Picture side: exam ready

2. Flashcard: almost there

3. Graphic organiser: understanding but low recall

4. Notes: starting out

KEY RETRIEVAL

Key individuals	Key dates	Key features
The 'Big Three' who met at Versailles were leaders from the USA, UK and France – Woodrow Wilson, David Lloyd George and Georges Clemenceau.	WW1 ended in November 1918 but the Treaty of Versailles was signed and agreed on the 28th of June 1919.	• War Guilt Clause, Germany had to accept responsibility for starting WW1. • Pay reparations to the allies. • Forbidden to ally with Austria. • Army and navy restricted. • Left out of League of Nations.

Key words	Key facts/figures	Key consequences
• Demilitarisation • Territorial • Reparations • Articles • War Guilt Clause • Rhineland	The army was restricted to 100,000 and the navy was limited to six battleships but no submarines. The reparations would be 132 billion marks! Land lost at Alsace-Lorraine was given back to France.	The people in Germany were shocked and angry, they felt the Treaty of Versailles was very unfair and cruel. This just made people hate the Weimar Republic even more too.

How it works: The focus of this task is for students to recall precise and essential core elements of knowledge. This can include key facts, dates, terms, quotes, statistics, concepts, effects, causes, characters, themes, individuals, turning points and so on. The headings provide guidance as to what students need to recall without providing any subject–specific prompts to keep the challenge desirable. It is useful for students to have awareness of what aspects of their course are key as this can help them with their independent study too.

Top tips: It is important with this task – as with all retrieval tasks – to allow for meaningful feedback and reflection. A class discussion and overview can check for any misunderstanding or misconceptions. During feedback I encourage my students to add any additional information in a different coloured pen.

KNOWLEDGE ORGANISERS

How it works: Knowledge organisers have become incredibly popular and widely used in recent years. Essentially, they work as a sophisticated summary of the core content and knowledge that students need to know. The tricky aspect of creating a knowledge organiser is to condense key information into one or two sides of A4. Although not easy for the teacher to do, it is useful as it allows for reflection and discussion with colleagues about content. Another reason information is condensed is to make this more manageable and less overwhelming than other resources such as textbooks can be. Knowledge organisers can be used across primary and secondary as well as different subjects. It is the information contained in the knowledge organiser that will form the basis for retrieval tasks and quizzes set by the teacher or created by the students for self-quizzing/testing.

Top tips: Collaborate with your colleagues when creating, designing and implementing knowledge organisers. They can be time-consuming to create initially but then they can become an essential classroom resource to support students. There are also plenty of examples of knowledge organisers online that teachers have shared freely and generously.

LEITNER SYSTEM

How it works: The Leitner system is a valuable way of using flashcards, combining retrieval and spaced practice. The focus of this system is to help students revisit the cards/topics that they have previously struggled with until they can retrieve that information with ease and confidence. This system does rely on students using their flashcards regularly for self-quizzing during the week so commitment is required, but we know effective learning is effortful. Once students have their flashcards on a Monday they will attempt to answer the questions and whether they answer correctly or incorrectly will result in which box the flashcard goes into. If students answer correctly the flashcard will go in the box labelled 'Box 2: Tuesday and Thursday', meaning they will return to the flashcard on Tuesday and Thursday. If the student cannot answer the question or provides an incorrect answer they put the flashcard in 'Box 1: The Everyday Box', meaning they have to keep repeating the flashcard every day to support the retrieval process. The following day students will repeat the process. If they can still not answer the flashcards from box 1 they remain there, but if they have now mastered that flashcard it will move to box 2. If students answer a question from box 2 incorrectly then it goes back to box 1. When students can correctly answer the questions in box 2 they will be moved to box three, only to be revisited on Friday. This process will continually be repeated, either with the same flashcards or for different subjects and topics.

Top tips: If you want to watch a great video explanation as to how this system can be used then check out the brilliant video 'The Leitner System' posted by Jon Hutchinson on YouTube. Jon shares how he uses the system with his primary class.

PICK AND MIX
(by Matthew Lynch)

Pick and mix recall challenge:

1: Guess who (is speaking)

'Go and look for the father of the child.'

'If she'd been some miserable plain little creature'

'It's better to ask for the earth than to take it'

2: Find and fix the mistakes

'Foul is fair and fair is foul'	
The thane of Fife is executed for treachery	
Macbeth's hamartia is greed	
The Gunpowder Plot was foiled in 1603	
The audience for this play is Elizabethan	

3: Give me three...

adjectives to describe Fred			
similes associated with Scrooge			
epiphanies Scrooge has			
items attached to Marley's chains			

4: On the other hand: Provide two different options on whether or not the pilot in *Kamikaze* is a coward.

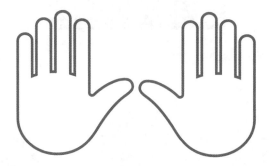

How it works: This idea, originally by Matthew Lynch, combines a range of suitable retrieval tasks for students to complete. All of the tasks mentioned are relevant to the subject and study of English literature and cover a range of areas from quotations to factual recall and elaboration. Depending on time, you could ask students to complete one task or two and then return to the other options next lesson.

Top tips: Pick and mix tasks can be problematic when the options are not desirably difficult. Students can opt for the easy task or skip straight to the challenging task which might not always be suitable. All of the tasks mentioned provide challenging retrieval without any gimmickry.

POST-IT NOTES

How it works: Do you love or loathe post-it notes? At one point post-it notes were a staple tool in my teaching and learning toolkit. I still use them in lessons and think they can be useful for low stakes retrieval practice. They are very versatile and the fact they can be easily disposed of and recycled adds to the low stakes nature of retrieval practice. Students can answer questions on a post-it note or write a mini-brain dump. Google Jamboard acts as a digital version of a whiteboard that students can add post-it note style responses to.

Top tips: It might seem unusual that I have included post-it notes as they are neither exciting or innovative in terms of a classroom resource. I wanted to include them as they have the potential to be used for effective low stakes retrieval. However, they can also be used ineffectively, as I have done in the past, as a gimmick or novelty task that doesn't support learning.

RETRIEVAL REFLECTION TICKET

Areas of strength/confident recall	Gaps in knowledge
• I can remember a lot of information about the Treaty of Versailles. I was able to recall the 'Big Three', the different terms of the treaty and how the German people reacted. I am confident about an exam question on this topic. • I am also good at remembering information about life in Nazi Germany, especially how life changed once Hitler came into power. I can give specific examples too about the roles of women, unemployment and propaganda. • I know the key dates, end of WW1, Treaty of Versailles, Wall Street Crash, Hitler coming into power and WW2.	• I struggled to remember much about the Weimar Republic, maybe because we did this so long ago? I need to go over the Weimar being established with the constitution, proportional representation and a basically that time period at the beginning. • I get confused between the Sparacist uprising and the Kapp Putsch. I need to go over that again. • I couldn't recall much about Gustav Stresemann. I need to look at that again.

How it works: I have been guilty of not providing enough time to my classes for meaningful feedback and reflection. This reflection ticket forces students to reflect on their areas of strength by writing their areas of strength and gaps in knowledge. What could they recall with ease and confidence? Which topics did they struggle to recall? Where are the gaps in their knowledge? This can be useful to refer to later to check if those gaps have been closed.

Top tips: I have found it very useful to skim through the responses, by doing so it addresses some common gaps in knowledge amongst the class that I can plan to act on. Identifying gaps in knowledge is useful for both the student and the teacher. It's important students also recognise what they can recall and that retrieval practice actually works!

RETRIEVAL REVISION MENU

Self-test	Flashcards	Past papers
Use your notes/textbook to create a quiz to self-test yourself.	Create a set of flashcards with Q&As, ready to test yourself.	Complete a past exam paper and use the mark scheme to self-assess.
Revision clock	**Brain dump**	**Mind map**
Break down the topic into 12 sections and complete a revision clock.	Complete a brain dump with as much as you can recall then check your notes to see what you forgot.	Create a mind map from memory, then check, review and add to your mind map.
Infographic	**Summarise**	**Retrieve, record & review!**
Create an infographic with sketches and notes from memory.	Write an overview of the key topics from memory then refer back to your notes.	Record yourself retrieving as much information as you can verbally then listen back and review.

How it works: Using retrieval practice in the classroom is great but what we also want is for students to be using retrieval techniques outside of the classroom and for the rest of their lives as lifelong learners! It can be tempting for students to resort to low utility and low effort strategies such as highlighting and underlining but we know they are not as effective. This menu can provide students and their families with guidance and support on how they can be revising and carrying out retrieval practice at home. The choice provided in the menu also promotes independence.

Top tips: I use this with exam classes and by the time I give students the menu they are familiar with the techniques included, as we will have already carried out most of these techniques in class. The menu can also be hyperlinked as a digital document so that if students want to access past examination papers the link will take them to the relevant site or to a blank template that they can download and use.

REVISION BOOKMARK

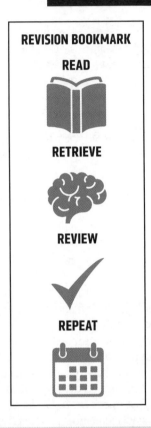

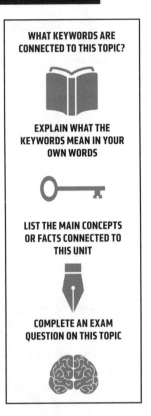

How it works: I created these bookmarks for my Year 10 tutor group but they can easily be adapted to be subject-specific. You can download my example above to share with your students using the QR code at the back of the book. The bookmark aims to keep students focused on using retrieval revision strategies outside of school. Parents have also found this simple explanation helpful too.

Top tips: QR codes can also be added so that students scan the bookmark and it will direct them to an online quiz, flashcards or past examination papers.

REVISION CLOCK
by Becky Green

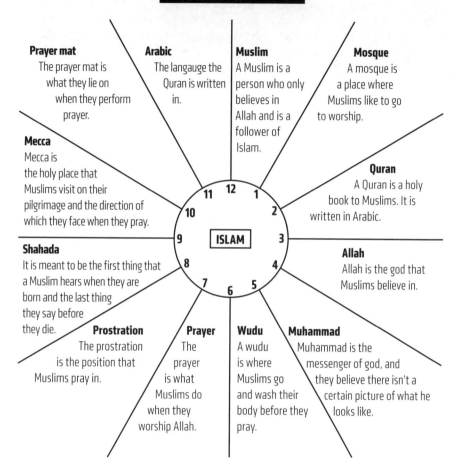

Prayer mat
The prayer mat is what they lie on when they perform prayer.

Arabic
The langauge the Quran is written in.

Muslim
A Muslim is a person who only believes in Allah and is a follower of Islam.

Mosque
A mosque is a place where Muslims like to go to worship.

Mecca
Mecca is the holy place that Muslims visit on their pilgrimage and the direction of which they face when they pray.

Quran
A Quran is a holy book to Muslims. It is written in Arabic.

Shahada
It is meant to be the first thing that a Muslim hears when they are born and the last thing they say before they die.

Allah
Allah is the god that Muslims believe in.

Prostration
The prostration is the position that Muslims pray in.

Prayer
The prayer is what Muslims do when they worship Allah.

Wudu
A wudu is where Muslims go and wash their body before they pray.

Muhammad
Muhammad is the messenger of god, and they believe there isn't a certain picture of what he looks like.

ISLAM

How it works: This activity involves breaking down a topic into small manageable chunks. The aim is to spend five minutes per section. This can be completed all at once, in a lesson or at home, or spread out over a series of lessons. This can be a consolidation task during the encoding stages but to make it a retrieval task it's simply no notes allowed!

Top tips: This has worked well with exam classes, especially with those students that struggle to structure and organise their time. Older students can be given a blank template and create their own headings using revision lists or specification lists. If completing on paper, A3 is better as more space is provided for each section. Visual images can be added to sections too.

SELF-QUIZZING

How it works: This activity can be done in a variety of ways. Firstly, if students have knowledge organisers they can use this to self-quiz by creating questions based on the organiser. Whether students use a knowledge organiser or not, they will need a lot of explicit guidance and modelling to know how to write a question that is desirably difficult – not too easy but not too challenging, as well as relevant to the content they are learning and genuinely provides an opportunity for retrieval practice. Quizzes can be created in class for students to refer to in another lesson and during that time forgetting can occur and the teacher can check over questions students have come up with. Self-quizzing can also become embedded as part of a homework routine too. Many schools provide students with exercise books specifically for self-quizzing. It is useful for the teacher to monitor this, not to track scores as retrieval practice is low stakes and workload friendly, but instead to hold students to account to ensure they are self-quizzing and doing so correctly.

Top tips: Explain to your students that self-quizzing/testing is very important because there will be many times, as part of home-learning, when revising or during higher education where they will not have the support of their teacher to prompt and encourage them. They will need to learn how to independently revise and check their knowledge and understanding of topics. Self-quizzing isn't easy but persevere!

QR CODES

Scan the QR codes below to take you to links to download free templates.

This is my website lovetoteach87.com. Here you can access all my blog posts about retrieval practice and teaching and learning.

www.lovetoteach87.com

This is my TES resources homepage. Here you can download my 'Effective study strategies' guide as well as templates to all my retrieval practice resources for free.

www.tes.com/member/K8SUE